By Robert Darrol Shanks Jr., PhD

Copyright © 2024 Robert Darrol Shanks Jr. PhD

Published by: Writers Publishing House
Printed in the United States

ISBN: 978-1-64873-539-4

All rights reserved. No part of this book may be reproduced in any manner whatsoever without written permission from the author except in the case of brief quotations embodied in critical articles and reviews

Cover Photograph entitled "Moon Bird", was taken early one morning in Williamson Valley near Prescott, Arizona.

The Power of Believing in God

And Other Stories to Stimulate Your Imagination

By Robert Darrol Shanks, Jr. PhD

Contents

AMERICA HAS STRONG ROOTS IN CHRISTIAN HERITAGE..................1

ARE OLDER CHRISTIANS MORE SUSCEPTIBLE TO FALLING AWAY FROM CHRISTIANITY? 5

A FLASH OF LIGHT AND THE SOUND OF A TRUMPET CALL PUT AARON'S WORLD INTO COMPLETE CONFUSION 8

FORTY CROSSES: *ARIZONA'S NEEDLESS BORDER DEATHS*..........20

HISTORY AND IMPORTANCE OF THE TEN COMMANDMENTS..........25

IS HEAVEN A REAL PLACE? 28

LEARNING TO FLY FROM THE GARAGE ROOF?..........31

LITTLE LEE-LEE'S TRASH BURNING CHORE ADVENTURE AND HIS NOTABLE CHEMISTRY SET ESCAPADE..........34

THE OLD AIRPLANE RADIO NEEDS REPAIR 37

READING ACADEMIC TEXTS CRITICALLY..........42

IMPORTANCE OF BELIEVING IN GOD AND GROWING UP IN A RELIGIOUS ENVIRONMENT........45

A POLARIZED AMERICA AND AN INEFFECTIVE CONGRESS REPORTED BY A WEAK MEDIA DISTRUSTED BY VOTERS......................49

WHAT ARE THE CORE BELIEFS OF CHRISTIANITY?.53

WHAT IS CHRISTIAN GRACE?........................55

WHAT IS SIN?........................59

WHEN WAS THE LAST TIME YOU READ THE U.S. CONSTITUTION? 62

WHY HAS AMERICAN PATRIOTISM DECLINED SO MUCH IN THE LAST 20 YEARS? 65

WHY IS CHRISTIANITY AND CHRISTIAN 69

GRACE SO MISUNDERSTOOD?........................69

THE POWER OF GOD'S AMAZING GRACE 73

A COLLECTION OF PHOTOS TAKEN BY BOB SHANKS 79

AUTHOR'S PERSONAL PHOTOS 114

REFERENCES 116

AMERICA HAS STRONG ROOTS IN CHRISTIAN HERITAGE

While not founded as a Christian nation, our country is deeply rooted in Christian values. Many of our founding fathers and their families migrated to the U.S. to escape the severe and often barbaric demands of European leaders who forced their populations to worship as they demanded. George Washington and other leaders at that time drafted our Constitution and Bill of Rights to ensure no religion would be a part of government. As one researches these historic events it becomes clear our First Amendment prohibited Congress from establishing a religious government. Article VI of the Constitution also clearly prohibits any kind of religious testing for serving in public office.

All citizens could exercise their personal religious freedoms as they wanted without fear of government controls and interventions. George Washington himself is reported to have said our government was not founded on the Christian religion. However, there is no single direct quote indicating Washington said this. The fact he signed a treaty with the Barbary States is an indication of his beliefs on this subject. These Barbary States treaties with Morocco, Tunis, and Tripoli were to prevent Barbary pirates from these northern African states attacking our shipping in the Mediterranean Sea. Before our Independence from Britain, the British Government protected shipping lanes in the Mediterranean and Atlantic oceans.

The question then rises to the surface of logical thinking, how did our country survive those rough early years? The answers can be traced back to the "Great Awakening" occurring during the 1730s and into the 1740s. So, let's examine this awakening just a little closer. Just what did this "awakening" entail?

Our founding fathers came to this country from a wide range of religious beliefs found in Europe and elsewhere, many were Christians along with countless other religious beliefs, and many believed that religion should only be kept at home or worshiped at a church. Our founders wanted to ensure that no religious influences could slowly migrate into public life. Research conducted in 2022 by the Pew Research Center[1] found that 60% of adults in the U.S. believe our country's founders wanted America to be basically a Christian nation, however, religion was to be kept totally out of government.

Additional research on the Internet, libraries, and other sources indicate many of our founding fathers seemed to be deists, a deist believes there is a higher power, there is a supreme being, but they believed God created the world and then left it to run and operate governed by natural laws. Deists for the most

---

[1] (Pew Research Center , 2022)

part rejected the idea of miracles, a Virgin Birth, and the Resurrection of Jesus. Deists also are resistant to organized religion. A delist believes in humans having free agency where they can choose their own actions and make their own mistakes. The term "deist" originated in England in the 17th Century and was popular among those who were in the educated classes of Europe. Even many Americans from a broad population range of education were deists as were the first three U.S. presidents during those early years of our country. In fact, historical research indicates Thomas Jefferson was a deist who reportedly removed all references to Jesus' divinity from his personal Bible. This fact can easily be researched using many historical texts available on this topic.

Despite all of the unpredictable times during our early years, after the founding of our country, we have survived and flourished. One could easily surmise our survival is directly related to how we were founded as a free country where citizens could determine their own religious beliefs and futures to make their own decisions right or wrong. The coveted and often misunderstood tenet of *"The American Dream"* is alive and well. Having stated this, we as Americans must all be aware of how our way of life and our freedoms are now constantly under attack and scrutiny by other not-so-friendly countries including other radical influences from our own citizens.

Our right as citizens to vote is sacred, should be revered, and protected, we must stay informed, we must vote, and we must be involved. We must guard against apathy and do all we can in our local community governments and Federal government to support our freedoms. Vote intelligently, this is your right as a free citizen of the United States of America.

ARE OLDER CHRISTIANS MORE SUSCEPTIBLE TO FALLING AWAY FROM CHRISTIANITY?

"Is not wisdom found among the aged? Does not long-life bring understanding?" Job 12:12

The scripture above should bring a sense of understanding to those of us who are growing older. One often hears the statement, *"If I knew then what I know now things would probably be a lot different."* Of course, not that many older Christians fall away from Christian faith, many enter into their later years deeply committed and active in their faith and church.

The reasons for falling away from their Christian faith can be very complex and unique to those individuals and should be handled with sensitivity and understanding. Many churches have special programs to reach older members with all kinds of support groups keeping them engaged and active. Research has shown that most Christian church members are between 50 and 60 years old. Many church members are probably over 60 years old. There has been a rather steep decline in church attendance in each generation within the U.S., perhaps those who drop out didn't attend Sunday School or church as children.

The loss of faith can be due to many life issues, such as the loss of a spouse, health challenges or other major life changes the individual has little control over. Some undoubtedly have a disillusionment with church internal politics for example. Perhaps there was some hypocrisy among church leaders and conflicts with the communities' relevant issues. One key activity to help with all of this is stressing the reading and study of the Bible as often as possible, daily, or at least three times a week. Getting involved in church Bible study activities and small group meetings, older Christians need to study various books on worship and other Biblical history studies.

Some who have lost their faith may be experiencing personal struggles, financial issues, medical issues, grief, mental health challenges, or physical traumas with the question "Why is this happening to me?" This is where sensitivity needs to be exercised with understanding and just being a good listener. Many older American grandparents are ending up as care takers for other family members' children, this can be difficult and is often a complex issue.

Aging issues often seem to move older adults into more worldly interests for some reason. One key method to help with all of these "aging issues" is volunteering to be a part of a church group that reaches out to those needing various life support issues. While not being counselors, those elderly individual volunteers have valuable life experiences and a sensitivity to the stressors of modern living. As often been said, *"I have been there and done that."*

Learning to be a good listener is extremely important, helping those who are older doesn't mean trying to "fix" their issues, but just being there as a friend and a good listener for those in need of support can be important and can make a big silent difference. Learning to pray for and with those in need regardless of their age is an important outreach activity for all Christians to undertake.

A FLASH OF LIGHT AND THE SOUND OF A TRUMPET CALL PUT AARON'S WORLD INTO COMPLETE CONFUSION

Aaron was suddenly thrust into a state of complete astonishment trying to understand just what was happening. His whole world seemed to be in complete disarray and made no sense to him. There was a sudden flash of light and a tremendous amount of noise like crowds shouting amid loud music like you would hear at a football game and then complete darkness for a moment before he could again see the world around him. The question came to his mind that perhaps there had been a nuclear explosion somewhere, were we at war? What is happening? It was strangely calm, with no wind but the sunlight seemed natural and ok. However, his little Nebraska town of 25,000 had derelict cars all over town, some had crashed into the downtown stores, and some were in the middle of the street still running with no one at the wheel! He heard a newscast on his car radio that there were plane crashes all over the country and apparently the world. Airports were in a complete panic; pilots had disappeared with copilots and other airline employees taking over and flying the planes. The huge flash of light suddenly became visible to the naked eye, the light seemed to be surrounding a figure that was part of the blinding light, the individual was dressed in white.

As more information began to come out about those who were missing, it was discovered they seemed to be all of the Christian faith and worshiped Jesus Christ as the risen savior, was this a coincidence, or indeed those being called home by God?

Aaron had read all of the "Left Behind" books. He also realized the popularity and interest in the concept of the Rapture was due in large part to those books. However, he now realized he was possibly in the real-life version, or how could all of these sudden disappearances be explained? He also realized, according to his mother's notes, that the term "rapture" doesn't appear in the Bible and only became something of an oddity to be explored by fiction writers in the mid-1800s. Aaron also sought out what is written in the Bible to find out what is said of Jesus' return and what will happen. Here's a brief explanation Aaron found in his mother's notes based on Biblical scripture.

In 1 Thessalonians 4:13-18 Paul is encouraging the believers in Thessalonica about their concerns of those who have died. He assures them that when the Lord returns along with a trumpet call the dead in Christ will be raised and those still alive will be caught up together in the heavens to be united with Jesus. Our Lord Jesus also teaches about his return in Matthew 24:30-31. He says all will see Him coming in the clouds at the trumpet call and His angels will gather the elect from throughout the world to be joined with Him. Because of these scriptures the term "rapture" was coined along the way to help describe these foretold coming events.

As Aaron walked up and down the sidewalks in his small Nebraska town, those residents still here had flooded into the streets to see why so many vehicles had crashed into each other, and why vehicles were left running with no one in them. The local barber also said he had several customers just suddenly disappear, the one man sitting in the barber's chair just vanished leaving only the cape used by the barber while cutting hair and was left tangling on the empty barber's chair. There was an air of panic as no one could explain what was happening. Newscasts on the radio and TV were full of reports of plane crashes, automobile wrecks, traffic jams, and complete confusion throughout the country and internationally. In many areas, the military and local police had to be called up in larger cities to get some order and organization to these disappearances and complete bedlam.

In Nebraska reports were that cars, trucks, and all kinds of vehicles just went completely out of control, crossing the Interstate Highway 80 medium rolling over, and crashing into other vehicles. News media said the scene along I-80 was completely bizarre. There were abandoned motorcycles, empty cars, and trucks left driverless and running, some had rolled over and were upside down, others just slowly coasted off the road into the weeds and fields. All of these vehicles were driverless!

Aaron dug out his cell phone and frantically called his mother, she had moved in with him after his father had died. There was no answer. He became worried as she had to be reminded to take her heart medicine. He jumped into his old restored 41 Ford Coup and raced home. Pulling into his driveway he saw his mother's car parked in front of the house. He rushed inside, but she was gone not a trace or note, the coffee pot was on and there was a cup of coffee and a plate with a partially eaten sandwich. What happened to her? Was she with this group of worldwide citizens who mysteriously disappeared? The burning question that was haunting Aaron was why didn't he disappear?

This strange bright cloud was sighted in the sky around the world and by citizens in every country during not only the day but at night as well. This apparently resulted in panic-buying and hoarding food and other critical supplies in some areas. Aaron's study of the Bible had helped strengthen him in times of stress. He often felt secure in reading God's word. He also knew full well that there is Good and Evil, and Satan did indeed exist. Aaron hadn't come to fully embrace Christianity, he still had not fully committed his mind and spirit to Christ, but he was headed in that direction. Was the great deceiver Satan behind all of the current turmoil trying to mislead the world? He didn't have time to find out, he wanted to find his mother, where could she have gone? Her car was in the drive as always and she needed to stay current on her heart medication. He contacted some of the neighbors, and they were just as mystified about the strange cloud and as confused as everyone about all of the strange events and worldwide disruptions, however, the neighbors still there said many in the neighborhood had disappeared from their houses and homes. Those still there had not seen Aaron's mother the last day or so.

Laying on the kitchen table was a partially written note, a list of items to pick up at the grocery store. The coffee cup was still warm to the touch as if she had just sat it down, but she was nowhere in the house. Aaron considered calling the police and reporting her as missing but all they would probably say was she had to have been gone for at least three days. They were undoubtedly confused about all the citizen disappearances as well. Aaron had just seen his mother earlier in the day as he left for work in his old 1941 Ford coup. He was only scheduled to work for a few hours that day at the hardware store.

Aaron's mind was still a-blaze with why he was still here, is this an invasion from other worlds? What did all of this mean? He was trying to become a good Christian so was this indeed the much talked about "rapture" so many Christians believe will happen despite the fact the term is not used in the Bible at all according to his mother?

Aaron tried to attend church occasionally with his mother when he could, he supported many churches sponsored activities, supported the youth programs, and worked diligently to help his mother as part of the church's mission program. He often listened to his mother read passages from the Bible in the morning before breakfast, she always picked a scripture in the New Testament to read. She also insisted on saying a prayer after each session. In Aaron's thoughts he was always impressed with his mother's ability to discuss each scripture and often looked up other relevant Bible passage details and was excellent at answering questions if there were any associated with whatever scripture lesson she had chosen to read or study with Aaron.

Aaron was also impressed with his mother and her involvement in her local church's "Life Group" where they actively discussed the Sunday sermon and scripture, was she with that group today? They often met here but it appeared Livvy was alone at home judging from the table and warm coffee cup. As Aaron's mind was in a semi-state of panic, the phone rang, he answered it and on the other line a very distraught female caller excitedly and very loudly said, *"Where's Olivia, I need to talk with her now?"* Aaron always called his mom "Livvy" as did many of her friends, but this individual said "Olivia" very formally. Aaron tried to calm her and explain as best he could that he couldn't find his mom either and was mystified about all of the upheaval and disappearances. The caller immediately burst into tears as she explained how Livvy was helping her to better understand the Bible and all of the promises of Christ and start attending church. He told the caller he would have Livvy call her as soon as she came home. The caller screamed, *"What if she has disappeared as so many have and won't be coming back."* Aaron had no answer to that question; he was just as puzzled as the caller about all of these strange events.

The book on the table about the rapture theory called "The Rapture Plot" conceived in the early 1800s was written by Dave MacPherson and was laying on the kitchen table along with notes about a discussion Livvy's Life Group had at one of her Life Group meetings. Another book on the table "The Rapture Concept" based in part on the Bible verse found in 1 Thessalonians 4:14-17 was laying on the kitchen table too. In that verse the Apostle Paul speaks of believers being "caught up" to be with the Lord Jesus in the air.

This reference to being caught up in the air, according to Aaron's mother, is a reference to the second coming of Jesus Christ. His mother's notes also stated the so-called Rapture is not, as some believe, a mythical secret arrival of Christ before a rapture as part of an end-of-the-world doctrine embraced by many Christians. His mother's notes from her Life Group seemed to emphasize that this concept is not accurate or intended to be interpreted or believed. All of this was new to Aaron, the more he read his mother's notes the more he found them to be fascinating. Many of her notes, referred to the book "The Rapture Plots" synopsis. Apparently, this is one of the texts being discussed in Livvy's Life Group. Aaron was so impressed with his mother's intellect and ability to read and research a variety of concepts. These skills of Livvy were probably due to her being an elementary school teacher for many years. Aaron was indeed quite proud of his mother but where is she? Her constant work to convince Aaron to attend church regularly with her and accept Christ was her ongoing job. While he was basically a believer, he had not totally committed himself to Christ, going to church and studying the Bible. This was very troubling to his mother, but where is she now?

Aaron raced out to look inside his mother's car for possibly some clues as to where she had gone, the car was as she left it the last time she drove it. However, while outside Aaron noted the light in the sky was still there and continued to glow brightly making the figure of this individual in the center of the light hard to distinguish. Was this an alien from another planet coming to Earth for a visit? News broadcasts indicated that people in every region of the world can see this amazing light in the sky. Finding nothing in her car he went back inside to read his mother's notes more closely that she kept in a journal about her Life Group discussions and scripture notes. Perhaps there was more to discover about his mother and where she might have gone within her notes.

Livvy had underlined and jotted notes about the book of Matthew in the Bible that stated the Son of Man will at a trumpet call send out angels to gather his chosen people from all nations and they will be caught up into the sky to meet Jesus. Her notes also included items from 1 Thessalonians where the Apostle Paul says Christ's return will be like a thief in the night, but all should be aware of the signs, earthquakes, diseases, and war among nations. Aaron thought to himself it sounded like the current news now. The onset of Covid 19 was, in his mind, a stark reminder perhaps we are living in the "last days" as predicted in prophesy. There were wars on every continent and region as nations seemed to have gone war crazy. Crime was seemingly out of control to some degree in every region of the U.S. and other countries as well. Was the initial flash of light amid loud trumpet-like music Christ coming to collect his chosen? Fear began to take control, so Aaron had to take some deep breaths and concentrate on not panicking. She may have just gone for a short walk. If only he had paid more attention to what his mother was researching, he wished in could go back in time and spend more quality time with her. But now, he just wants to find out where she has gone!

Suddenly the light in the sky began to brighten and expand as there was a stream of other individuals beginning to appear with the individual as the light brightened and expanded. The individual in the center of the light could now be seen quite clearly, it indeed looked quite similar to the many pictures and artistic renditions of what Jesus Christ may have looked like. The light had expanded into an extremely bright cloud-like affair covering almost the entire sky when suddenly it began to shrink and then just disappeared. Aaron was completely in a state of shock. In his heart and mind, he seemed to know he had just witnessed the second coming of Christ. He now seemed to know where his mother had gone! Aaron, for some strange reason, now had a complete peace of mind as if he knew where his mother was now.

Aaron quickly went inside and turned on the television news, it was flooded with images taken from all over the globe of this strange occurrence, indeed, all people worldwide witnessed this amazing event. But as usual, the mainstream media tried to play down this occurrence as a possible alien invasion geared to taking large portions of the world's population for whatever nefarious reasons. Of course, those who were left in many churches and knowledgeable about scripture were quick to correct this obviously very weak spin on the event. Many, calling themselves Christians were dumbfounded and in an almost state of shock as to why they were still present and had not been taken up.

Political turmoil was brewing as many in key government leadership positions were gone, where possible, those in chains of command, however, were quick to step up as replacements. In the news, current wars soon seemed to intensify as many new outbreaks were now occurring in the Mideast. Israel was now under heavy attack and was being bombarded by neighboring countries that had not been openly hostile until this event occurred. In major U.S. cities, new waves of crime were increasing taxing police forces to their limits. Police stations had initially been flooded with missing persons reports but that was subsiding, police everywhere indicated they had no rational reasons for the disappearances and had wholesale losses of personnel. In some areas, governors had to call up the National Guard to help restore order, but many units had lost key leaders and manpower causing all kinds of problems similar to what the police in many cities were experiencing.

The moral fabric of the U.S. as well as in many other western countries was being shattered and degraded each day. One of Aaron's favorite books was George Orwell's satire, "Animal Farm". It seems to him that it was now happening in many respects throughout the country and the world as more and more control locally, nationally, internationally, and at the state level was being used to control situations due to the many disappearances, Aaron felt like he was now living in an Orwellian nightmare.

Orwell's book was a dark warning about the many dangers of totalitarianism, it was written as a satire about Russian's communistic brand of government and the Russian Revolution. In the novel a group of farm animals take over their farm planning to run it as equals, however, the leaders take advantage of the less intelligent animals and now are the oppressors. As they increase their power, it becomes a very oppressive force. The dogs in the satire are symbols of how the government can use police and military force to control society.

Now that the police and military was being used to control and counter the rise in crime and loss of key leaders, the population that is left is beginning to feel the controls as over reactive and negative. Due to the loss of key personnel some manufacturing and whole farms had gone vacant along with crippled critical supply chains. All kinds of restrictions are now being put into place by the government; the rationing of food is being planned along with other restrictive measures against excessive movement and use of energy.

Aaron turned off the news, he had heard enough and came back into the kitchen and quietly sat down at the table, his mother's partially eaten sandwich and now cold cup of coffee were stark reminders, he knew his world would never be the same again, his future now seemed aimless.

His mother's notes lay off to the side of her cold cup of coffee as he read her last entry taken from the Bible's Revelation 22:21...

"When we reach heaven, we will not boast about what we accomplished on earth. We will sing about the grace that saved us, sustained us in every trial, met our every need, secured our safe passage to heaven, and granted us

the privilege of seeing our Savior face to face. Grace abolishes every human tendency to bask in self-glory, and it causes us to give God all the glory for what He has accomplished in our lives."

FORTY CROSSES:
Arizona's Needless Border Deaths

The busy traffic zoomed around the eleven Christians as they silently marched down the side of the Pan-American Highway in Douglas, Arizona moving slowly and deliberately toward the border. Curious on lookers walking and in cars slowed and stared as each Christian stopped and held up a small white cross and said the name of the deceased individual that the cross represented, some represented undocumented remains of unknown individuals, and some were children. The crosses are often placed against the curb in silent testimony to these needless deaths. The sight of these forty crosses stretched out for over two blocks in the setting Arizona sun evoked a lot of emotion. Only forty crosses represent the hundreds of deaths that often occur along our southern Arizona desert border with Mexico!

Various estimates indicate well over 10,000 people died in the past 1990's decade estimate in their attempt to cross the border. Of course, in 2024, the trek from the south into the U.S. has gotten even worse, according to the U.S. Customs and Border Protection. One estimate indicated that in 2023 over 8,000 people died trying to cross the US. Mexico border. *This has been called a minimum estimate as not all deaths are reported. Most likely the deaths are much higher now since our entire southern border has been invaded by millions of illegal aliens in 2024. The open-border concept is not working and will not work.*

Do we need to deport all illegal aliens so our country will be like all other countries with protected borders? Do we need strict protocols for those from other countries visiting or coming here to live? All legal procedures should be followed if an individual from another country wants to live in the U.S..

The small white crosses laying against the curb of the Pan American Highway in Douglas, Arizona are mute reminders of the hundreds of needless deaths that take place in our desert as our neighbors set out on the dangerous trek from Mexico to the U.S. hoping for a better life and income for their families. Every year the deaths along the border are setting records.

At this writing, a mother died three miles east of Douglas with her two children at her side, a twelve-year-old and his four-year-old brother. Some of a local pastor's congregation and friends supporting the church found the boys hugging each other and crying at a U.S. Customs check point. The children were waiting to be sent back to authorities in Mexico.

Healing Our Borders (HOB) is a Douglas Arizona, Agua Prieta Sonora-based, interfaith group that has been actively praying for all migrants for over 20 years, especially for the families of those who have needlessly died in the desert and for families that have not heard from loved ones and do not know their whereabouts or conditions. HOB delivers blankets and other items needed by migrants. This ministry also cleans the deserts and lands of items that are left behind by these migrants in their desperate journey for a better life. The HOB group tries to educate people on both sides of the border about the dangers of trying to trek across the desert. For many, coming from deep within the interior of Mexico, such as the tropical Chiapas State where they only know the jungle can't understand a desert with no rivers or lakes. More illegal immigrants are coming from even farther south in the Americas.

Many southern border Christian churches are involved in missions for Christ along the border. As Christians, we are to make disciples for Christ and get the good news of salvation out to the world despite politics.

Entering the U.S. illegally, or re-entering after being deported, is a crime under federal law with penalties ranging from fines and up to six months in prison for a first offense, or fines and up to two years in prison for subsequent offenses or re-entry after deportation.

HISTORY AND IMPORTANCE OF THE TEN COMMANDMENTS

As one is growing up one of the first learned concepts, whether taught by parents or learned at school, is the Ten Commandments. As a young boy growing up in Grand Island, Nebraska, I have a very vague and distant memory of attending a Sunday School class in an old church. As part of a program, I believe for parents, there was music and a parade of small people who resighted memorized scriptures and displayed their colorful drawings. I just vaguely remember having to stand up in front of the congregation with other little people to recite our memorized verses. I was probably about 4 years old and not in school yet.

The old church was close to the very old red brick two-story Howard Elementary school that was built in 1884 for $20,000 which was a lot of money in the 1800s. I attended Kindergarten there in the mid-1940s. The school was bordered by the streets of Sycamore, Kimball, Fifth, and Sixth Streets. I only have very vague memories of the school. I remember the floors all creaked and groaned as students walked on the old wooden floors. I don't remember when I had to attend another school as I grew older. However, I do remember the building had two attached metal tunnel-like affairs for students to slide down from the second floor in the event of a fire. Sadly, the building was condemned by the State Fire Marshal in 1951 and demolished. The area was turned into a park.

In those days students learned a variety of history, some of it of course came from the Bible. Though there was and always will be a strict separation of church and state, it is hard to disconnect the two as one examines the rich history of our country. In that era, no one, or few disputed what was taught in school and the mixture of Biblical and American history, this is my memory accurate or not.

The 1956 movie, "The Ten Commandments" starring Charlton Heston has a special memory for me as it seemed to make my faith in God come to life and give me more of a direction in what I was to do in life. I graduated from high school in 1959, so the movie was not that old and was still quite popular.

Trying to visually duplicate what is written in scripture is monumentally difficult and open to much criticism from many religious writers and authors, however, the film's special effects at that time were quite difficult and yet amazing for the era, the movie did win one academy award.

Another movie filmed in 1959, "Ben Hur" is another Biblically based film with an equal number of special effects and a special message about believing in God. Research into these movies indicates putting a date on Moses's life is almost impossible. Was the Pharaoh Seti I Moses's adoptive father? This probably is false as is the supposed love triangle between Moses, Nefretiri, and Rameses. As usual, Hollywood filled in the gaps in Moses's life from many imaginative writings that have appeared over the years from a variety of sources. These movies often depict the Judeo-Christian mission as similar to the U.S. trying to bring "freedom" to the world and do not really have anything to do with ancient Egypt, however that is how the entertainment business in Hollywood operates.

An interesting side note: the painted eyes and the exaggerated makeup used in these movies are probably not that far off from being accurate as the ancient Egyptians did use heavy make-up and did paint their eyelids, lips, and nails. These movies do and can give a little more insight into Biblical scripture whether one believes in God or not.

IS HEAVEN A REAL PLACE?

There are lots of Near-death Experiences (NDEs) and remembrances of going someplace outside of our known world where it was indeed beautiful and idyllic. There are many books available on this subject. Research on this topic has indicated that one in ten people have had NDEs and returned to report what they had seen and experienced. While your author is not among the NDE group, there is a fascination about this topic, especially for those with terminal illnesses and parents who have lost children. This author has lost two of his children and often thinks of them every day. My wife has also lost two of her children from a previous marriage. So, we both often grieve together on birthdays and holidays. The discussion about Heaven as a real place often comes up as we both are interested in this topic. Let's take a brief look at this topic.

To begin this brief discussion, I must make it abundantly clear my wife, and I are Christians and attend church regularly, read and study the Bible daily, and are a part of a wonderful local church. Without this strong faith in God, Jesus Christ, and the teaching found in the Bible, we would not be positive and forward-looking to the future, no matter how uncertain it looks and despite the heart ache we have endured losing children.

Authors Randy Kay and Shaun Tabatt, in their book, *"Stories of Heaven and the Afterlife"* have made it their mission to interview those who have had NDEs. This is just one book of many on this topic. Their interviews cover a wide range of topics from those who experienced not only seeing heaven but hell as well. Many who have had NDEs have experienced major changes in how they now live their lives.

One must also accept the fact Biblically there is a Hell as well and is documented in the Bible. If one is familiar with Dante's book "Inferno" about hell one comes away with a frightening realization about the concept of Heaven and Hell. In this age where Christianity and religion are often unfairly trivialized, this writer was drawn to Biblical teaching and a hunger for more knowledge on the subject. This is where faith enters the picture, most Christians have a strong faith in the word of God and realize the fact there is a Heaven and Hell. There are so many references to the concept of heaven and hell in the Bible.

What is the main objective of this short essay then? Simply, find a good Biblically based church where you can study the word of God, and realize the power of prayer. Make a difference in how you live and sort through all the political "noise" of our current age and the persecution of those who believe in God and Jesus Christ. I haven't included a list of Bible verses but don't take my word for it, prove it to yourself, open the Bible, and start researching some topics.

LEARNING TO FLY FROM THE GARAGE ROOF?

Many in the younger generation have always been interested in and fascinated with flying. In talking to those in the aviation industry one discovers a lot of future pilots and those working in all phases of aviation started with model airplanes as well as reading exciting stories from past flying adventures.

This author's family was no exception. My two younger brothers were both in military aviation service, my brother Don was an inflight H-3 helicopter mechanic in the Air Force, and my little brother Larry worked on Navy fighters in the field of electronics. Later in civilian life both of them owned their own small private airplanes. My brother Don worked for United Airlines as a mechanic retiring from the California Air National Guard and United Airlines as well. My brother Larry went on in the field of electronics working for several different companies. My sister Vicky was a reserve Naval nurse as well as a Veteran's Hospital nurse. This writer also served in the Air Force as an intelligence analyst and later as a USAF Air War College professor.

My uncle Ben and my dad both wanted to learn to fly and kids in that era often built go-carts from junk, but they instead decided with a bunch of other boys to build what they thought was an airplane that would fly and launch it from the garage roof. This was a time before youth became hooked on the small screens of phones, computers, and television. Reading aviation magazines and literature about flying was a form of entertainment as were movies at the theatre about flying.

Apparently, as the story goes, this so-called airplane contraption had plywood wings and a tail. Too bad there was not a picture taken of this wooden creation. The wheels were from an old baby buggy. How they got the plane up on the roof of the garage was a feat. They apparently tied a rope to the tail so it would stay on the incline until launching time. My uncle was the pilot, so he positioned himself in the front of this heavy plywood and two-by-four framed plane. When ready he signaled to release the rope and down the side of the roof went this plywood winged wonder. It of course crashed with a loud thud into the ground, throwing my uncle clear and, in the process, breaking his collar bone.

My dad was an enlisted troop assigned to a P-39 squadron in the Aleutian Islands near Alaska during WWII after clearing the islands of enemy Japanese soldiers. My uncle went on to fight in Europe in the Army and helped free a concentration camp in Germany. They were a part of the greatest generation and sparked our family's interest in serving our country in the military.

This story also brings to mind the old movie series "The Little Rascals", one could see these little "shorts" at the Saturday movies for .15 cents before the main movie started. My grandfather was a projectionist working in the booth above the audience running the very large 35 mm old film projectors of that time. And of course, for a lot of youngsters, there were always a lot of books and magazines about flying to read as well.

Our modern communication system devices, phones, laptops, television, and large desktop computers have diminished and stolen the delight of learning in some respects, often learning the hard way sometimes about what would fly or not. Life may have gotten too easy for our youth of today and I often shudder to think of how some of our young men and women would do if needed again to defend this great country of ours against a world-wide aggressor. As a country, we must continue to pray and seek God for personal guidance.

LITTLE LEE-LEE'S TRASH BURNING CHORE ADVENTURE AND HIS NOTABLE CHEMISTRY SET ESCAPADE

Little Lee-Lee was the youngest boy in his family so the chores his two older sisters didn't like to do were always given to him. Raking and cleaning the back yard was one of those chores. As he was raking the ground and cleaning up the back yard and then burning the trash in the large barrel, he saw an old hair spray can his sisters had used laying on the ground so he just tossed it into the barrel to burn with the rest of the paper and trash not realizing aerosol spray cans should not be burned!

Leaning over the barrel as he stoked the fire, there was a loud explosion. Of course, the spray can exploded. Little Lee-Lee was engulfed in smoke, sparks, and flames. He staggered back dazed. As he stumbled into the kitchen from the back yard his face was covered in black soot, his eyebrows were singed along with his hair just above his face. He looked like a character from a movie or cartoon. Lee-Lee's family and sisters were of course terrified. His appearance had the entire family horrified but then they all exploded into laughter as they understood he was ok, just dazed, and frightened. His soot covered face was indeed quite hilarious.

Lee-Lee was a typical boy of that age, interested in how things worked and full of eagerness to learn and experiment. This was before the age of personal computers, and cell phones, so what was often learned was by trial and error, reading books and magazines at the library to find out new information in science.

That was also the era where a variety of chemistry sets were available for parents to buy for their children. Many parents often had items that could be used to mix up rather dangerous and questionable mixtures. In those days of the 1950s, there were no stringent regulations on many things that we face today. We now all have to be aware of the many local, state, and national governmental regulations that are in place regulating our lives.

Lee-Lee also had quite an interest in explosives so he often would retreat to the basement area of the family's home in the Chicago area to experiment with his chemistry set. As usual, Lee-Lee was interested in making something different, so he set out to make a stink bomb.

The family often gathered in the kitchen area near the entry to the basement. As they were sitting around the table, they all suddenly smelled something horrible emanating from the basement. Little Lee-Lee had quite successfully concocted his stink bomb. It was a cold blustery typical Chicago day as everyone temporarily retreated to the outside. They all came back in and rushed around the house, opening windows and doors, starting some fans trying to get that horrible smell out of the house. Everyone quickly put on coats as well because of the cold Chicago weather.

Many families who have older daughters often quickly discover that boys can be a different matter to raise. Some families are often not prepared for how boys learn, which is often quite different than girls. One parent experiencing these different behaviors was heard to say, *"My daughter never did any of those things"* as they questioned what their young son was doing that terrified his older sister.

Behavioral data over the years has shown boys can often have some early troubling behaviors with what is called "externalizing behaviors" resulting in aggressiveness or destructiveness whereas girls show "internalizing behaviors" such as anxiety but also show more competence and caregiving behaviors. Families can have quite an interesting mix of sibling rivalry along with all the other behaviors just mentioned.

One can quite easily surmise that it is critical to have both parents working together to raise children in a family.

THE OLD AIRPLANE RADIO NEEDS REPAIR

It was just another day in Victor's workshop. His task today is to take out an old aircraft radio used for communication in an old long ago restored WWI Sopwith Camel. Someone, years ago, had installed the radio in the old Sopwith WWI airplane hangered at the old airport. The vintage WWI airplane was going  to be put on display at an airport but now the owner wanted to get it ready to fly again, so he needed the radio to function properly.

The British Sopwith F. 1 Camel shot down more enemy aircraft than any other Allied World War I fighter according to various Internet research. The Sopwith Camel is famous because it had such unmatched maneuverability, however, although the camel was difficult to defeat in a WWI dogfight. *Tricky handling characteristics, however, made the Camel a dangerous aircraft to fly. The fighter had 90% of its weight in the front half of the plane, giving it a very unnatural feeling when flying it due to its unusual nose--heavy flying characteristics. However, the Sopwith Camel was a superlative fighter aircraft of WWI and is reported to have shot down over 1200 enemy aircraft, more than any other Allied fighter of that war. Over 5000 were built between 1916 and 1920.*

The Sopwith camel had a number of engine variants. Many of the engines of that time did not have throttles so they were at "full throttle" while the ignition was on. The only way to "throttle back" was while the engine was running the pilot would use a selector switch cutting the ignition off to some of the cylinders thus reducing power for taxing and landing.

Victor had heard there were strange stories about this plane. The old vintage WWI airplane was stuck in a little used storage corner of the old hanger and no one wanted to work around it or even be too close to it. Strange voices had been heard coming out of the cockpit. At night, there supposedly was a weird glow coming out of the plane, so no one ever wanted to work at night in the hanger.

Victor didn't give those stories much credence and besides that he didn't believe in ghosts and hauntings. However, that was about to change. He positioned the radio in the center of his work bench, poured a cup of tea and laid out his tools ready to tackle why this old tube operated radio that had been converted to solid state and computerized but didn't work. One problem was it was missing the electrical cord so he couldn't plug it in to his work bench aircraft battery power source. He cut a length of wire and attached a plug so he could get some battery power to the old radio. As he opened the back of the old dusty case, to wire up the power cord, out fell an old yellowed and crumpled scribbled note:

"Forgive me for being so angry at your disappearance," the note went on to say, "I still think there's been some mistake, and I keep waiting for God to fix it ... Forgive me for not knowing how to protect you from death." What a strange, crumbled note to be found inside an old aircraft radio. The note was yellowed with age, apparently it had been there a long time. It was as if whoever placed this note within the radio case was

hoping somehow the message would get out to whoever owned the airplane at the time. It seemed like an anguished cry of terror and helplessness. This cryptic message posed many questions for Victor as he worked on the old circuit board.

As he got the radio to start warming up and appeared to be getting power, the little workbench speaker suddenly came to life with crackling noises and what sounded like distant voices amid the sound of gunfire. The voice on the speaker sounded like a pilot flying the airplane but in distress. There were sounds of engine and wind noises as the voice tensely said, *"I need a heading to get back to base"!*

Victor was visibly a bit shaken as he dashed into the center of the hanger looking for the old man mechanic, Sean, who knew everything there was to know, it seemed, about WWI airplanes. He wanted someone to verify what he was hearing and besides that, Sean was also the mechanic who was working on the old airplanes 130 horse power Clerget rotary engine trying to get it running again. "Hey Sean", Victor shouted out across the hanger floor, "I need you to see this." Sean slowly limped over; the old mechanic had been wounded in WWI in one of his legs and it healed badly causing him a slight limp. Victor said, *"I'm confused about this old radio that's in the Sopwith Camal."* Sean said he would be of no help; all he did was work on engines, but Victor insisted. As Sean entered the electronics shop, he could also hear the strange crackling noises and voices coming from the old radio. All he could say was *"Where are all those voices coming from Victor?"* Victor simply said, *"I don't know Sean, it's as if someone is flying the old Sopwith Camel. "As you know Sean",* Victor said, *"These planes didn't have radios during WWI so what are we hearing?"* Both seemed stumped and amazed at what they heard coming from the little old aircraft radio. As suddenly as the radio came to life, it stopped and fell silent. However, radio and plane were now repaired and functioning.

A wealthy investor was visiting London and heard of the Sopwith Camel restoration project taking place in northern England. As soon as the airplane was in flyable condition this unidentified individual purchased it for an undisclosed and rather outrageous sum of money. No one is sure where the airplane is today. However, there is one known Sopwith Camel still in flying condition. According to Internet searches, the only airworthy Camel is registered as **ZK-SDL** and is owned by The Vintage Aviator Ltd in New Zealand. The Sopwith was disassembled and shipped there in 1930 and is supposedly still in flying condition today. Could this be the Sopwith of this story?

There is one replica Sopwith Camel on display at the National Museum of the United States Air Force located at Wright Patterson AFB, OH and is pictured above.

READING ACADEMIC TEXTS CRITICALLY

What is "Critical Reading?"

Critical reading is careful, thorough, thoughtful, and active reading. It is not scanning, skimming, or quick reading. It is "college reading"--the kind of reading you are expected to do in college courses. You are involved in critical reading whenever you are interested in a textbook, and you make a variety of comments about it as you read it.

One can scan the page headlines and sub heading highlighting these along with the first sentence of each paragraph (usually the topic sentence of a paragraph). Then return to the beginning and start reading for information, taking notes in the text or notebook as you go. Some students prefer reading the selection first then rereading it again and then taking notes. What's comfortable for you?

Critical reading means you take the time to think about what is on each page you read. Your reading must be active: passive reading, in which you simply read a text with no marking or discussion of it as you read, rarely sticks in the mind very long and very often is a waste of your time and ultimately the instructor's time. Even if you take notes and never look at them again, you are twice as likely to remember what you have read because you have processed the text actively.

It should be obvious that you cannot write well about what you do not understand, but many people make the mistake of not reading a text completely, missing class discussion of it before a paper or a speech is due or just rushing through the textbook assignments without really comprehending it fully. One cannot write well either if one cannot read effectively.

Active, critical reading usually involves marking the text, so you need to have a printed copy to mark (even if only with pencil marks you later erase), or you need to write comments on paper using a system to note the page and paragraph or line number in your text. Active critical reading is not just the highlighting of important passages. It is that and much more, as an example, you should write regular margin notes as you read your text. Such notes can include brief succinct comments explaining your agreement or disagreement with important points, comparisons and contrasts to other texts or ideas, and new ideas that occur to you.

As part of your active reading strategy, you also should stop at least briefly after each page you have read. Then take some notes if you haven't already as you were reading. Then at the end of each page, you also should ask yourself, *"Have I understood everything on this page?"* A student's active reading strategy will more than often require reading the assignment as a minimum at least twice; for some subjects and texts one may have to read the assignment and associated notes many times for a clear understanding.

You should be able to write a brief, one or two-sentence summary of what the page says -- and if you haven't yet written a note for that page, summarizing it can be your note or notes. Just looking at sentences and turning pages does not constitute critical reading. Critical reading means actively comprehending what you have read and intellectually digesting what is on the page.

Another step in engaging in critical reading is to actively engage the text right after you have read it once. This means talking with others about it, putting the words into practice, making an alternative model of what has been discussed (for example, a short story or a drawing), or a simple note about it.

Take the time to become an active reader by taking notes as needed for understanding and digesting in your mind key points from the reading assignment. Work at becoming a better reader.

IMPORTANCE OF BELIEVING IN GOD AND GROWING UP IN A RELIGIOUS ENVIRONMENT

Psalms 71:5 says, *"For you have been my hope, Sovereign Lord, my confidence since my youth."*

Social scientists today have confirmed the benefits for children growing up in a religious environment according to Dr. Pat Fagan, the director of the Center for Research on Marriage and Religion. He is also a senior fellow at the Marriage and Religion Research Institute in Washington, D.C.

After compiling the findings of over 100 independent social scientists conducted over twenty years on the effects church attendance has on the lives of kids, Fagan said, *"When policymakers consider America's grave social problems, including violent crime and rising illegitimacy, substance abuse, and welfare dependency, they should heed the findings in the professional literature of the social sciences on the positive consequences that flow."* This quote is from Rob Kerby, in *"Church Kids Less Likely to Divorce or Live in Poverty"* This quote is from an article that can be found at *beliefnet.com.*

Social Science research conducted over the years has clearly shown that learning at an early age that there is a God, and that each person is made in His image provides a healthy atmosphere for well-adjusted children. In the Bible, Joseph and Mary furnished a home centered on God's love, His commandments, and His way of life, which is undoubtedly one reason God selected them to provide for His Son's early childhood development.

Sociologists, in researching parental desires for teaching their children about God and the importance of the church were surprised by some of their findings. Sociologist Christian Smith writing for Christianity Today[2] found that religious parents in the U.S. all talked very similarly about why they wanted to raise their children in a religious environment, the researchers thought they would find a lot of differences and diversity but in all those interviews the parents all basically said the same things, even Buddhists, Muslims, Hindus, and Mormons all had similar understandings about religious parenting. Christian Smith and his colleagues conducted over 200 interviews.

While these interviews were conducted primarily with youth and what they believed, the interviewers soon discovered that a close study of parents was needed as well. Apparently, many in the general public often think parents just take their kids to church to have the church take care of teaching religious doctrine and training, however, those conducting the research found that parents for the most part felt their main job was instilling in their

---

[2] (Christianity Today, 2021)

children their beliefs and importance of specific religious training. Researchers found parents wanted church and Sunday school to be a safe general resource for religious training for a sound grounding in the power of believing in God.

While we all know the world and our American families are much more diverse than any of our experiences can accurately convey. Society is constantly changing in our current tumultuous times and is affecting family life in so many unforeseen ways. Family research also indicates there is a decline in the "nuclear family" as a firm foundation for sound mother and father parenting and raising children with basic Christian disciplinarian guidelines. Research findings also indicate a decline in church attendance is troubling as well.

The question then seems to be how can one be faithful to a belief in God while at the same time grappling with all these changes and differences that seem to be flooding into the lives of all families. Has American religion evolved into such an individualistic and consumer-based reality? Religious authors and ministers have to come to a grip on how to handle all these societal changes, and yet not sell out to becoming a wimpy-like sectarian, just a member of a group with a particular set of interests such as is found in many religious groups swaying and bending to whatever current adaption is coming within these "religious" group's systems of belief. Unfortunately, there are few if not many places left in our world where sectarian strife and conflict do not exist these days, especially it seems in all the many American mainstream churches with various evolving interpretations of Christian Biblical teaching and learning. All American Christians should realize the power and importance of prayer.

Religion is often more openly under attack so finding a good sound Christian church steeped in traditional Biblical teaching is getting more difficult. The politics of disparaging those who are Christians may indeed only worsen as our uncertain future unfolds in America.

A POLARIZED AMERICA AND AN INEFFECTIVE CONGRESS REPORTED BY A WEAK MEDIA IS DISTRUSTED BY VOTERS

The nature of U.S. politics historically has always been highly charged, it seems to this writer that many American schools, colleges, and universities have forgotten to read and learn from our history for a common-sense understanding. I remember tough partisan debates during the 1980s and then after all the tense and sometimes bitter contentious debating the opposing parties would often get together after the day was over in a social setting as friends to discuss the outcome.

Now, opposing political parties have developed high levels of anger at each other and often resort to negative name-calling. This angry name calling is doing nothing but widening the negative partisan polarization between the party in control and the opposing party.

This polarization also bleeds out into the news media, who don't often report very factually. Some news outlets spin the results in favor of one party or the other. This spin can have negative effects for voters, often causing bitter feuds among friends and family as sides are taken and for what purpose?

Polling results indicate that more Americans seem to believe the other party is misguided and are evil people. There seems to be a culture of contempt for each other in American politics.

How does the public get their political leaders to build bridges so effective legislation can get passed that benefits all citizens in the long run? The media has not helped this negative polarization affect at all in these bitter divides. Our political leaders should be encouraged to work together, building bridges across the conservative-liberal divide so our country can move forward positively.

Some recent polls indicate Americans have an extremely low view of the media. It's almost like we have a media ghetto in the U.S. The poor condition of journalism has to bear a lot of responsibility for stoking polarization by not reporting the news fairly and objectively. Some news outlets border on being propagandists for one or the other party.

This writer has a B.A. in journalism and often has felt that if his past college professors were still here, they would be completely horrified at what has happened to journalism whether it be electronic media or print. So, what can be done about this?

Getting letters off to congressional and senate leaders is a starting point as well as letters to the editors of various publications. Polls also indicate most Americans trust their local and state governments to fairly handle problems. However, there is an extreme distrust in our federal government. A very low opinion exists concerning the U.S. Congress.

Perhaps a Non-Governmental Organization (NGO) can band together with other NGOs to rank the most objective and fair national news media outlets and produce some kind of Objective Reporting Guidelines for verification and reporting both sides of all news. Of course, our sue-happy world causes all kinds of legal problems with this idea.

The use of the Internet and now all kinds of streaming services has also muddied the water. As a former college and university professor, I used to tell students to adequately verify writing assignments and other academic tasks using at least two sources, however, now depending on the topic multiple sources should be required. Our media has to bear a lot of responsibility for not adequately reporting all the news correctly and fairly without bias.

Should a list of guidelines and/or media commandments be developed to ensure proper reporting for all news outlets? There is already a set of principles developed by the Society of Professional Journalists[3] (SPJ). They have four principles for all ethical journalists to adhere to for integrity.

The SPJ Society declares these four principles as the foundation of ethical journalism and encourages their use by all in media.

---

[3] (Society of Professional Journalists SPJ, 2014)

Unfortunately, there are no teeth or methods to ensure that these four principles are adhered to; they are: **1. Seek the Truth and Report It; 2. Minimize Harm; 3. Act Independently; and 4. Be Accountable and Transparent.**

As stated earlier in this article, our media bears a lot of responsibility for governmental polarization in this writer's mind by not objectively reporting the news fairly. Our elected leaders need to be held responsible as well. There is too much influence from lobbyists and other special interest entities. Congress needs to make decisions in the best interest of all Americans, not the lobbyists and special interest groups.

WHAT ARE THE CORE BELIEFS OF CHRISTIANITY?

Using the information super highway, the Internet, one can find a lot of information about almost every kind of subject or topic. Caution must be emphasized here that lurking in the shadows is AI, if that is even possible for Artificial Intelligence (AI) that really isn't a Sensient being, to really lurk in the shadows! The power of AI is evident in many google searches on topics and various subjects. However, a major caution would be to thoroughly vet any information using more than one or two Internet sites, especially if the topic is controversial.

When still teaching at the university level I always emphasized students use multiple sources on certain topics being researched for articles, presentations, and research papers and to question all information as well as to be hyper-critical about information if something doesn't seem quite right. If some information looked suspicious, it most likely was not entirely accurate or possibly misleading.

When preparing to write this short article on the core beliefs of Christianity, the Internet sites (many of course AI-driven) yielded a lot of useful accurate information. The core beliefs are *A) There is only one God who is perfect, omnipotent, existing as a Trinity, the Father, Son, and Holy Spirit; B) The Bible is God's word; C) Jesus is*

God's son; D) Jesus was both fully human and God; E) All have sinned; and F) Mankind has salvation through faith in Jesus Christ who was sacrificed for all.

Christians also believe that love is a fundamental characteristic of God and that all people should love God, love their neighbors as themselves, and be able to forgive and love their enemies. All Christians should value respect for others, and that mankind was created in God's image. All should have hope and a confident expectation of life. Christians also know they can get to know God through prayer, fasting, and giving.

Christians should project love and be an example for others by how they live. While conversion to Christianity is important for unbelievers to realize, it cannot be forced upon those unwilling to accept what it has to offer. One of my favorite expressions over the years has been *"You can't hit people over the head with the Bible."*

WHAT IS CHRISTIAN GRACE?

Go to just about any Christian church anywhere in the U.S. or the world for that matter and you will hear the term "Grace". As a young person growing up in Nebraska and attending church and Sunday School, I was always confused about this term. The term was used so interchangeably with other terms and still is today. For this writer, my Sunday School teachers just assumed I knew what it meant, but I really didn't know for sure. I was shy and afraid to ask many questions when a young learner. So, just what is Christian Grace? We must first realize that at the heart of trying to understand Grace is Jesus Christ.

To begin this discussion about Grace let's look at the definition. Grace as used in our Christian Belief is the free and unmerited favor, and salvation of God for our many transgressions or sins through Jesus His son's sacrifice for all our transgressions. Grace is God's honored gift to mankind. *Romans 2:24, "We are justified by his grace as a gift, through the redemption that is in Christ Jesus."* These are God's gifts that are free and undeserved by all people. Many pastors have described grace in terms of the power of God working in us to give us a transformed life if we accept it. Grace can also be defined in three ways, *prevenient, justifying, and sanctifying.*

Prevenient Grace

This phrase has been used to describe grace given by God preceding the transgressions of a sinner exercising saving faith in Jesus Christ. This term is from a Latin word meaning "to come before, to anticipate." It has also been described by theologians as "irresistible grace". This short article is not meant to be a deep theological discussion of grace but simply to inform the reader there is a lot that goes into the study of grace by theologians and those who want to enter the ministry. Be prepared to do some research and delve critically into the word of God in our Bible.

Justifying Grace

Justifying grace is a term used to identify the grace by which God freely pardons and reconciles a repentant sinner to Himself. This phrase is primarily associated with the Wesleyan tradition, though the concept is not unique to John Wesley's teaching. Before going on one asks the question, who was John Wesley? John Wesley (1703–1791) was an Anglican (old English Church dating to the second Century) evangelist, theologian, and co-founder of what is now the Methodist Church. Wesley was born in the small English town of Epworth in England and was the fifteenth child of Samuel and Susanna Wesley. John's father Samuel was an Anglican priest.

Sanctifying Grace

Sanctifying grace is a supernatural gift from God that makes a person holy and pleasing to God. It's also known as the *"grace of justification"* because it makes a person acceptable before God. Many church beliefs say sanctifying grace is believed to be given through baptism. The study of grace reveals the goals of all graces from God, which are to save us, make us holy, open our hearts to God, and ultimately allow God to give us eternal life.

Now that we have established a basic understanding of Grace, let's move on to a discussion of what was just mentioned above, Grace is Jesus Christ and is available to anyone who believes in these words found in John 3:16, *"For God so loved the world that He gave his one and only Son, that whoever believes in Him shall not perish but have everlasting life."*

For this writer, those words bring to my mind the old John Newton song, "Amazing Grace, How Sweet the Sound That Saved a Wretch Like Me."

(Newton was an English evangelical Anglican minister.) Stop and think about this for a moment *"…he so loved the world he gave his only son for the redemption of all peopled".* For parents, their children are everything so to even think about sacrificing a child for others is a hard concept to grasp and understand but there it is, this gift is from God for all people. When double-checking this scripture, and cross referencing it with other Bible translations, it becomes clear this is an undeniable truth passed down over the last two thousand years in countless interpretations regardless of the ethnic origins and various religious adaptations. As a reader, verify this to your heart's desire and remember, Jesus Christ gave His life for all of us.

If this short article has piqued your interest, contact a local church, or find a good reliable Christian Church through prayer and attend services to find out the many and diverse benefits that await your mind and spirit only a Christian understanding can provide.

WHAT IS SIN?

When one is reading the Bible or other religious publications, the word "Sin" is mentioned often. Perhaps a more detailed description should be undertaken even if the word is more or less universally understood.

The actual definition of sin is any action, thought, or word that is considered immoral, shameful, selfish, and goes against God's divine laws. This concept is central to many religions including Judaism, Christianity, and Islam. *

Different cultures also have their own interpretations of sin. The Bible defines sin as going against God's standards. The Bible's original language defines sin as missing a mark or target. Theologians divide sin into "actual" and "original" depending on its gravity. Sin is also defined as disobedience.

Because of Adam's transgressions and sin of rebellion, he was sentenced to spiritual death and that was passed on to all humans. King David in Psalm 51:5 stated, *"Surely I was sinful at birth, sinful from the time my mother conceived."*

There are three types of sin, <u>*inherited sin*</u>, as King David said in Psalm 51 above, <u>*Imputed sin*</u>, and <u>*personal sin*</u>. Imputed Sin is sin attributed to us and all mankind from Adam's guilt. His sin is credited to all humans. Most people have never thought of "sin" being this detailed and all-encompassing.

Inherited Sin

This sin belongs to us all. When Adam first sinned, his inner nature was transformed as a result of his rebellion. His spiritual death and depravity were a direct result of his original sin that is now passed on to all humans who came after him.

Imputed Sin

To impute is "to take something that belongs to someone and credit it to another's account", to actually steal from another. After Adam's sin, everyone was subject to death, even before the Mosaic Law was given, because of this stolen sin, our standing before God was in jeopardy. This is why Jesus Christ gave his life, to redeem us all from Adam's sin.

Personal Sin[4]

Personal sin is that which is committed every day by every human being. Because we have inherited a sin nature from Adam, we commit individual, personal sins, everything from seemingly innocent untruths to murder. Those who have not placed their faith in Jesus Christ must pay the penalty for these personal sins, as well as inherited and imputed sin. So now we can choose whether or not to commit personal sins because we have the

---

[4] (Questions, n.d.)

power of the Holy Spirit who dwells within us. When we do sin, the Spirit convicts us (Romans 8:9-11).

Once we confess our personal sins to God and ask forgiveness for them, we are restored to perfect fellowship and communion with Him.

"If we confess our sins, He is faithful and just to forgive us our sins and cleanse us from all unrighteousness" (1 John 1:9).

We are now condemned three times due to inherited sin, imputed sin, and personal sin. The only just penalty for this sin is death, read (Romans 6:23), not just physical death but eternal death (Revelation 20:11-15).

Thankfully, inherited sin[5], imputed sin, and personal sin have all been crucified on the cross by Jesus, and now by faith in Jesus Christ as our Savior *"we have redemption through His blood, the forgiveness of all sins, according to the riches of His grace" (Ephesians 1:7).*

---

[5] (Google , n.d.)

WHEN WAS THE LAST TIME YOU READ THE U.S. CONSTITUTION?

Talk to just about anyone who is a citizen or who came to our country as a legal immigrant or even those who came illegally but want a better life personally or for family, they often more fully understand our country's rich history than many of our own citizens.

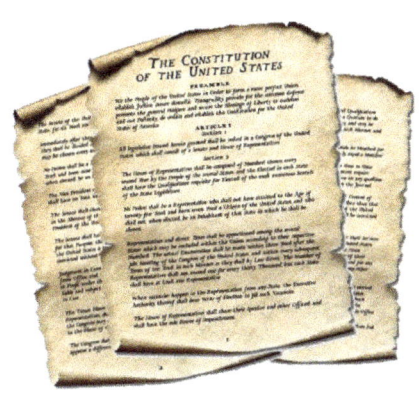

And yes, we have the good, the bad, the ugly in our past 250-year-old history. We are indeed a young country in many respects.

Many immigrants have a better understanding of our Constitution than regular Americans. All immigrants are striving for the American Dream and know we are indeed a unique country in the history of international relations. That is why so many people from around the world immigrate to our country legally or illegally. And at the heart of all of our freedoms, too often taken for granted by many Americans, is our United States Constitution. When was the last time you picked up a pocket-sized copy and read it over?

When stationed in the country of Albania when serving in the USAF, a former communist-run country, I was assigned to work out of the U.S. Embassy and the Albanian Military Ministry of Defense (MOD), I noticed each day our Embassy was open for local citizens to have access, there was always a long line of people waiting to apply for a visa to come to the U.S. Some days the line stretched for blocks. Unfortunately, in this writer's mind, our public schools, colleges, and universities don't do a very good job of teaching civics and our Constitution, if it is taught at all anymore. Do some checking where you live, what will you find? Most likely your answer would be one of disappointment.

Turning Point USA's Charlie Kirk, who spoke here in Prescott, Arizona recently, has developed a very easy-to-read Constitution. Each section of Kirk's Constitution has a list of terms with definitions well explained since our English language now is not the same as when the Constitution was first framed and written by our founding fathers.

If you would like a copy, go on-line to Turning Point USA, and get a copy, read it, and check out the terms as explained. When teaching at the university level I always had a small copy of the U.S. Constitution in my brief case, especially when teaching International Relations and working with students who were attending from sometimes as many as 40 countries.

If those of you reading this and have attended some of the parades held in downtown Prescott, Arizona, you will always see historically dressed individuals honoring our local and Arizona State history. The fact newspapers in the U.S. can cover a whole host of topics, with no governmental interference is due to the U.S. Constitution. Get a pocket-sized copy and read it.

WHY HAS AMERICAN PATRIOTISM DECLINED SO MUCH IN THE LAST 20 YEARS?

This author's memories of growing up in Nebraska are full of patriotism, while in elementary school, saying the Pledge of Allegiance every morning at the beginning of each school day facing the U.S. Flag. When in junior and senior high school the pledge and the music from America the Beautiful were often played  over the school's intercom throughout the school during home room and before classes started for the day. Every classroom usually had an American Flag on display. The burning question is what happened to this wonderful spark of patriotism honoring our country that was so ingrained into our educational system?

Could be as many Christian writers believe, that part of the problem is the breakdown in the family unit, poor church attendance inadequate and weak educational curriculum selections, and lack of, or no sound civics and American History classes. In this writers' opinion, no civics classes are a part of the American History curricula at all in public education. These points serve as an excellent starting point for more of a discussion.

Further research into this topic has also discovered a shocking decline in teaching the development of U.S. democratic institutions, freedom, and prosperity. Our American history has a rich background of our founding father's hard work and planning to build a free and functioning society for the benefit of all citizens.

In November of 2023, the Center for American Institutions at Arizona State University[6] published a report on U.S. History courses offered at over three dozen American universities.* This was a year-long study that uncovered some grim realizations that history is not being taught but instead that American history is full of racism, oppression, violence, greed, exploitation, failure, and an overall national decline.

The survey also uncovered some concerning statistics that more than sixty percent of history course syllabi used politically charged terms from identity politics. Terms emphasized were "white supremacy", and "toxic masculinity". What's alarming is the emphasis on gender roles, homosexuality, queer theory,

---

[6] (News, n.d.)

militant social protest, and various forms of how citizens are victimized. The report showed that there was no sound well-researched political history, and military history was largely absent from nearly every syllabus that was reviewed. Most courses reviewed did not address military operations in World War I or World War II. They focused on the home front, racism in civilian and military life, and the suppression of civil liberties in wartime. Diplomatic history is likewise neglected, as was the invention and the growth of business and industry and how our worldwide business development occurred launching the U.S. into being a worldwide business leader. Instead, many courses emphasized black nationalism, militant feminism, and the suppression of civil liberties in emergencies and during wartime.

The overall trend and emphasis on the primary mission of the study of history in this survey was the correction of today's social problems. *Over the last twenty years, the number of students graduating with a history major has dropped by fifty percent, according to the survey and report.*

During the same period of this survey and report, many universities removed history surveys — Western or World History and U.S. History — from their general education requirements for a Bachelor of Arts degree. History courses that were once the cornerstone of a liberal education have degenerated into platforms for politically motivated negatively charged political partisan grievances. All of this is reflected in the decline of enrollments in history as they have shriveled away and the wonderful and unique history of our nation and the principles that have shaped that history go unlearned.

One recommendation from this Arizona State University survey and report was to create new degree programs that are more welcoming to intellectual diversity based on sound historical research. How this is to be done nationally remains to be seen and is a monumental task few schools and universities would choose to undertake. As stated in the report, "teachers and professors should be obligated to provide students a full understanding of the entirety of American history" but this report does not say what authority should compel them to meet that obligation. Until we resolve that question, it appears real reform in American History curriculum development will remain out of reach for many American students[7]. Below are some historically dressed citizens in a Prescott, Arizona, fourth of July parade.

---

[7] (The American Crises, 2023)

WHY IS CHRISTIANITY AND CHRISTIAN GRACE SO MISUNDERSTOOD?

We have established the definition of Christian Grace: Grace is God's honored gift to mankind.

Romans 2:24 clearly states, "We are justified by his grace as a gift, through the redemption that is in Christ Jesus."

These are God's gifts that are free and undeserved to all people. Many pastors have described grace in terms of the power of God working in us to give us a transformed life if we will but just simply accept it. Grace is an undeserved gift to all from God, it's unmerited and unearned existed before a person was born and is not related to any action a person may make. Romans 11:6 clearly states it is undeserved and free, a clear concept in Christianity and Judaism. So, then the question has to be asked, why does it seem that Christian Grace is so misunderstood?

Perhaps some of the problems are with the various religious denomination's interpretations of the Bible. Review some of the various religious church groups methods of worship and one soon finds many types of worship procedures and methods not seemingly related to any Biblical interpretations and methods of worship. There is a deep divide between the Catholic Church and many protestant methods of worshiping God. Study the life of Martin Luther and one soon finds many issues between Catholicism and Protestantism. Why did this happen? What does all this mean?

These questions have no easy and quick answers, but some general reasons begin with some individuals thinking grace is a reduction in God's expectations, that of course is not so, scripture is the source for true understanding of God's expectations. Many readers don't fully understand what grace means relative to understanding justice and forgiveness Biblically. Along with this line of thought, it is evident most people do not understand the power of prayer either.

One strange source of not fully understanding Christian grace is AI, yes Artificial Intelligence! When AI accessed the Internet and Google on this topic, there was an abundance of information about why Christian grace is not fully understood. Let's take a quick look at this un-seeming source of AI-generated data from multiple authors.

AI Overview

- Confusing Grace with Cheapened Law: Some peoples mistake grace for a reduction of God's expectations, which can lead to a low view of Christian standards. This can cause people to believe that God's standards are attainable and that they can do what is required of them.

- Misunderstanding Justice: Some people may not fully understand the grace and mercy that God has given them and may be driven by a misunderstanding of God's justice.
- Fear of Vulnerability: Grace can be scary because it requires people to be vulnerable and authentic with themselves and others about their beliefs and indeed how they may live.
- Misunderstanding Trust: Grace can be terrifying for people who have been sinned against, due to a misunderstanding of grace, trust, and forgiveness.

Personal works

Personal works can hinder grace, as they focus on doing what God has called us to do in our own strength and power, rather than God's.

In the Christian faith[8], grace is generally defined as undeserved favor that is freely given by God to anyone who believes. A basic tenet is that people are saved through Christ by faith through grace.

---

[8] (Google , n.d.)

All this writer can say is to find a good Christian church with a strong youth program and study the Bible daily. Pray daily and often for God's guidance and forgiveness for human nature always comes up short of the glory of God.

THE POWER OF GOD'S AMAZING GRACE

Countless hymns have been written over the years to praise God, but *Amazing Grace* stands out in history as a simple hymn that has changed the lives of many and still has a vital impact today on those searching for answers about life. The lyrics are simply written about the power of forgiveness, mercy, and redemption, the turning away from evil. The hymn was penned by a former slave trader John Newton in 1772 and published in 1790. While there are over 20 melodies associated with this hymn, probably one of the most recognizable tunes is the simple melody from American composer William Walker's "New Britain" for the words in Amazing Grace[9]. Here's the simple yet powerful words:

Amazing grace, how sweet the sound
That saved a wretch like me
I once was lost, but now I am found
Was blind, but now I see
'Twas grace that taught my heart to fear
And grace my fears relieved
How precious did that grace appear
The hour I first believed

---

[9] (Christianity.com, n.d.)

Through many dangers, toils and snares
We have already come
'Twas grace has brought us safe thus far
And grace will lead us home
When we've been there ten thousand years
Bright, shining as the sun
We've no less days to sing God's praise
Than when we've first begun
Amazing grace, how sweet the sound
That saved a wretch like me
I once was lost, but now I am found
Was blind, but now I see

John Newton didn't fully embrace the power of believing in God and accepting Christ as his savior for many years after his narrow escape from death at sea. He didn't pen the famous words to Amazing Grace until many years later. Sailors were not particularly noted for good behavior or manners. Newton had a very bad reputation for profanity, being course and rude, his life was full of debauchery and supposedly his behaviors and language even shocked many sailors. His life is quite a mixture of both good and bad behaviors. He was a very rebellious young man who chose to live a life on the sea. As one delves into his life it becomes evident, while in his youth, he was a very dislikeable individual with a strange patchwork of life experiences.

Even after he became a believer and worshiped God, he was still transporting slaves in chains, his life is indeed puzzling and quite troubling. He did later become a mature Christian, a pastor, writer, and a strong crusader against slavery, this turn around is really remarkable and quite admirable. The grace of God was indeed powerfully displayed in the life of John Newton. In later life this man from Britain knew where he was going and tirelessly worked for Christ and the belief in God our eternal father. His words have helped many an individual accept Christianity and move into a life of Chrisian service.

An Arizona Baptist pastor, Whitney Walters in one of his sermons, told a story about a famous person on a train trip in central Europe. The individual was Albert Einstein. On the train the conductor was coming around to punch the tickets, when he got to Einstein, who he immediately recognized, Einstein couldn't find his ticket. The conductor said that was okay as he recognized him, and he was sure he had purchased a train ticket and not to worry about finding it. As the conductor made his way back through the passenger rail road car he notice Einstein was still looking for his ticket and again told him not to worry about the ticket. Einstein's reply was he needed to find it so he could remember where he was going! Indeed, do we know where we are going?

In summing up Newton's life, one can produce a few key points. First, it is easy to see the priority of conversion to Christianity and transformation of a person's messy life becoming a servant of God and teaching the power of Christianity's life-changing affects to others. The second point to consider is to understand we cannot save ourselves; we are all sinners and only God can transform us from a wretched life where we are lost and blind. Only Christ can save us. The third point is understanding the conversion is a process that necessarily does not occur over night but can be long and protracted as in Newton's case. Yes, there can be dramatic sudden conversions with wonderful results, but for some the journey to accepting Christ can take years after the seed is first planted in a person's mind. Faith can blossom and grow into meaningful Christian service slowly for some people. Some admit their failures and say to themselves, *"I will do this tomorrow, or I can't now but I will later. It has been said that tomorrow is the devils and today is God's Day."* The power of redemption should not be put off.

Newton indeed received a large amount of grace and while it took many years for that to flower into meaningful service to others, we must realize as we witness to others, acceptance and saving grace should not be put off, we all are lost and blind, but Christ can and does save and transform anyone's life. Newton died at 82 in 1807 just months after slavery was ended in Great Britian.

Christ can give us all a rich amount of grace so we must all work to share it with others using whatever gifts the Lord has given us. Newton turned from a wild life of rebellion and sin and became a senior statesman for Christ in Britain proclaiming the gospel and changing the lives of many for over two hundred years as a result of his song.

It has been recorded that John Newton's last words were simply, *"My memory is nearly gone but I remember two things: I am a sinner, and Christ is a great savior."* Even today, his song, *Amazing Grace* has a powerful message for all who sing the song or hear it.*

John Newton

A COLLECTION OF PHOTOS TAKEN BY BOB SHANKS OVER THE YEARS.

These photographs were all taken by
Bob Shanks unless otherwise noted.

Cambridge England memorial U.S. Cemetery

Bob Shanks in white hat rafting in Colorado.

F-100 Thunderbirds over historic Mildenhall England church.

Albanian hero Skanderbeg taken near Tirana, Albania.

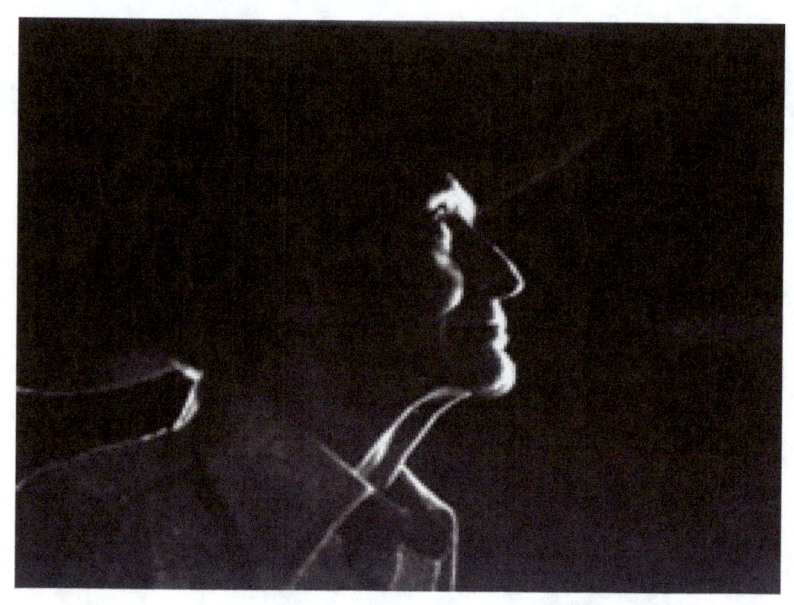

Old timer taken at Stuhr Museum in Grand Island, NE.

A Rumble seat from a past era.

Western Heritage Celebration: Blacksmith reenactor taken at Sharlot Hall Museum, Prescott, Arizona.

Old locomotive engine, Stuhr Museum Grand Island, NE.

Rifle cleaning, RAF Mildenhall

Snowy wind mill Sandia Mountains in Albuquerque, NM

Fall colors in the mountains near Flagstaff, Arizona.

Full "Strawberry Moon" as seen from Prescott, Arizona

Prescott, Arizona Air show, B-17 with Red Tail P-51 escort.

B-17 flyover for the Love Field Airport Air Show in Prescott, Arzona

Reenactment of a WWII parachute jump at a Prescott, Arizona airport air show.

A radio-controlled model fly-over of a WWII P-39 fighter.

Windmill Snow and Granite Mountain, Prescott, Arizona.

Reenactment of a WWII parachute jump: Prescott, AZ Airport airshow.

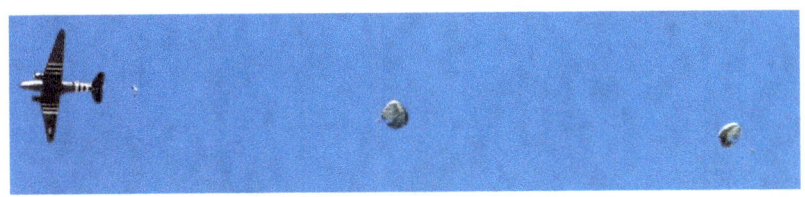

Embry-Riddle Aeronautical University student landing at Prescott, AZ airport.

Bobcat just out strolling.

Arizona cactus flower.

A rescued Bald Eagle at the Prescott, Arizona Zoo.

Parachute jump over Prescott, Arizona's Love Field Airport during an Airshow.

Prescott, Arizona: "Everybody's Hometown."

A painting by Dana Cohn and Julie Hutchins in Prescott's Whiskey Row Alley.

Prescott Arizona's Watson Lake with Flagstaff, Arizona mountains in the background.

Summer sunset in Williamson Valley, Arizona near Prescott, AZ.

Bobby Kennedy Photos taken in Grand Island, Nebraska in 1968, three weeks before his untimely and very unfortunate assassination.

Radio controlled model airplane taken in Chino Valley, Arizona at Chino Valley Flyers Flying field.

Revolutionary war drummer in Prescott July Fourth parade.

Prescott Arizona parade participant.

Prescott's historic and patriotic reenactors.

Prescott's historic and patriotic reenactors.

Prescott's historic and patriotic reenactors celebrating our rich U.S. heritage.

Uncle Sam visiting Prescott Arizona.

Prescott July Fourth Parade participants.

A Clydesdale Horses in Prescott July Fourth Parade.

A patriotic passenger in a restored 1940's pickup truck in a Prescott, Arizona parade.

Prescott's Arizona's Christmas City Acker night.

Reenactors in a Prescott, Arizona Fourth of July parade celebrating Arizona and U.S. military history.

A street in Lima, Peru.

Images above are from Williamson Valley near Prescott, Arizona

AUTHOR'S PERSONAL PHOTOS

The author served in the U.S. Air Force right out of high school first as an enlisted Still Photographer and then eventually moving into photo reconnaissance work as part of the Air National Guard and USAF Reserve components. After four years' of active-duty service, he then attended college using the G.I. Bill, getting his B.A. in journalism. He also has an M.S. and PhD in Curriculum Development from the University of Nebraska. He taught journalism and photography at the junior high school level while also serving in the military reserve component, getting his commission as an officer in 1980 and eventually retiring as a full Colonel.

While doing his enlisted service he was assigned to support the base newspaper while stationed at RAF Mildenhall in England. He won several awards for his photography while serving in Europe as a photo journalist. So, he has a portfolio of photographs from his various jobs and assignments both in the military and civilian world, some of his photographs are included in this section.

The author also served as an adjunct professor teaching part time at Northern Arizona University (NAU) and Embry- Riddle Aeronautical University (ERAU) in Prescott, Arizona.

REFERENCES

Christianity Today. (2021, June 21). Retrieved from ttps://www.christianitytoday.com/ct/2021/june-web-only/parenting-kids-teens-pastors-cross-wires-purpose-church.html

Christianity.com. (n.d.). Retrieved from https://www.christianity.com/church/church-history/john-newton-discovered-amazing-grace-11630253.html

Google. (n.d.). Retrieved from https://www.google.com/search?q=why+is+christian+grace+so+misunderstood&sca_esv=d8162cf97d98a7d0&sxsrf=ADLYWIKi0y15Xcr-Xdx6PkOKFWltUeKBVQ%3A1725793791260&source=hp&ei=_4XdZpq2Db28kPIPmMG-wAk&iflsig=AL9hbdgAAAAAZt2UD1gHveLGxt7JBD6tjL7hN2zCnX96&oq=why+is+&g

Google . (n.d.). Retrieved from https://www.google.com/search?q=what+is+%22sin%22%3F&sca_esv=9783522cabc36d5f&sxsrf=ADLYWIK-y8lUoaZ8iNb769IC3F9y4CAxMA%3A1726056741027&source=hp&ei=JInhZsG7PK_nkPIPk9GewAk&iflsig=AL9hbdgAAAAAZuGXNYqw0oT84r04T58MUPPxjADFWydp&ved=0ahUKEwjB3aK37rqIAxWvM0QIHZ

News, A. F. (n.d.). Retrieved from https://azfreenews.com/2023/11/new-report-shows-college-american-history-classes-focus-mostly-on-social-justice-revisionism/#:~:text=By%20Corinne%20Murdock%20%7C%20Center%20for%20American,conclude%20with%20a%20depiction%20of%20America%20as

Pew Research Center. (2022, Oct 27). Retrieved from https://www.pewresearch.org/religion/2022/10/27/45-of-americans-say-u-s-should-be-a-christian-nation/

Questions, G. (n.d.). Retrieved from https://www.gotquestions.org/imputed-sin.html

Society of Professional Journalists SPJ. (2014, September 14). Retrieved from www.spj.org/ethicscode.asp

The American Crises. (2023, Novemberq 17). Retrieved from https://americanideal.org/report-exposes-failing-u-s-history

www.ingramcontent.com/pod-product-compliance
Lightning Source LLC
Chambersburg PA
CBHW072211070526
44585CB00015B/1286